Implacable Art

ANNA MENDELSSOHN

Other books by Anna Mendelssohn (Grace Lake) from Equipage:

Viola Tricolor

Bernache Nonnette

Tondo Aquatique

Implacable Art

ANNA MENDELSSOHN

FOLIO · EQUIPAGE

PUBLISHED BY FOLIO AND EQUIPAGE

FOLIO

PO Box 202, Applecross, Western Australia 6153
PO Box 937, Great Wilbraham, Cambridge PDO CB1 5JX United Kingdom

EQUIPAGE

c/o Rod Mengham, Jesus College, Cambridge, United Kingdom

First published 2000

Printed and bound in the United States of America by Lightning Source

Typeset in Swift 9.5 / 13

*The publisher is grateful for the financial assistance of the
Judith E. Wilson Fund, administered by the Faculty of English,
Cambridge University, and of the Performance Writing Programme
at Dartington College of Arts.*

British Library Cataloguing-in-Publication Data
A catalogue record for this book is available from the British Library
ISBN 1 876857 00 5 paperback

SP

1 3 5 7 9 8 6 4 2

for my parents, Morris & Clementina,

whatever the eternity, life losing its love is tarred by reduplicated heresy
entertaining the angle of readership that agrees to enjoy disconnected rêverie
where the old cannot speak as fast and furiously, life having cheated them
of desires, of changes in the very fabric of their lives, crushed. crushed
in some sort of heaven that exists elsewhere yet exists without substance.
others' children walking around each other, a paper cone for filtering the ink through its tip.
a pretty burst of dance, rhythm making me lose orthography, yet I fight for it
back & hear the slide in love and wonderment lost at the memory
of my parents' dancing. and wonder why their memory has been crushed
in the new bourgeoisie's determination to ascribe everything filthy to be
below the belt which is the green shoot of crossed signals.

Im Gewitter der Rosen

Wohin wir uns wenden im Gewitter der Rosen,
ist die Nacht von Dornen erhellt, und der Donner
des Laubs, das so leise war in den Büschen,
folgt uns jetzt auf dem Fuß.

INGEBORG BACHMANN.
Piper München Zürich.
Sämtliche Gedichte. p. 66.

Acknowledgements

'that is what you are told' and the English version of 'à la France' were first published by *Involution* in 1996.

from   Implacable Art.

In unlike minds soft verdancy
reconnoîtred for barrack room politics
....
....
When the fat coca-cola man lands
on you in the night, fling open
the shutters and yell for Paint,
Sheet metal, burin & copper wire.

messages left for, changing for dinner, the bearers,
a roman sea, the touff of decline, arp, palette, sovereign,
patriotism, matriotism, dull, undisturbing. carmen 99.

running at chantilly. dressed for the morning. white shoes.
soft invitation. cards back from the printers. gold italics.
small houses can be roomy when time is occasionally. carmen 2.

not one voice. a little girl walked off smiling & killed herself
by dropping the wooden beam she had been carrying
over her falling body. We all Look alright. carmen 19.

hanging tiddlers in a row on a string line. safety pins.
canes in the shallows. blue silk for aleksandr's speech to
the wobbling greasy hot never mind no talking in cinemas carmen 5.

retiring, redounding, zuyderzee bite eye cheekbone
two or one jump down practising first world war homesickness,
same old grouse over too much see what is not adjacent carmen 4.

to the school playground & winston churchill's sensible comment,
money does not rule a young runaway on an international flight
to a wadi, textbook in hand, fighting over one violin & a manuscript. carmen 42.

Staged whispers.

a beginning weighed running startled experience
dragged from the gynaecium mouthed by pretence
irregular simulacrum in master hands
moulding little women in crotchety barns
indirectly revolution meant trust in validity
not weak & easily influenced word perfect lads
and sisters heavily practising jesuitry for subtlety's sake
accumulating pats on the back from big brothers;
the Chair, in a deadly stylized sclerosis may be
Inhabited by half a gnat, folly, in a three-cornered
warning that furniture is what makes the Egypt of the Englishman.
A woman uses syntax like a broom sweeps across an old fortress
A man snaps backwards, walk, walk faster, he has heard—
the march militant and although old cannot grow
Out of temptation to discipline his salvation
He has been instructed to expunge poetry, to uproot trees,
so he takes a woman to be his charge & later apologises
for knowing no tradition, for syphoning turpentine in ballet shoes,
for hiding in the used car tip,
for having no sense of depth
and even less of dimension,
for confusing gum with gouache, and ash with the grate's
carbonized pre-history, woolly & probative stesichorus
it's all been run through, the academies have been decoyed
by womb snatchers on time release, to give the economy last.

in **medéa mé**, dismounted, dead country, "it's a risk," has to Pronounce
the initiative annunciated, tell memory tell the past understatement.
was socially "known" in umbrage. awarded against, wallflower
spooled back to lictorage, "it could have been correct," the tower
coleridge guarded me akin to ancient leaves against relayed interviews
of masks applauded by black nights of schott sequins on iced stone,
steady; another twelve races adjacent, notice smooth, templar
white drinking vessel, a mug shot for a serillian word, must I? must?
must I thump my breast, before stepping over the kerb, must I be curbed?
so that bearing the scars of dementia I enter by a secret crack
black and scarlet to the bite on a splendour cruise into hygiene
that the telephone is there, & my heart has lost its mouth.
waiting with their scalpels, pulling out kilometres of fine intestinal
ducts, sired, squaws squandered, ah! this will reach the majority's
house, in the old part of town, where the garden moistens underfoot
fingers filed to points, never see, converts to a tight lipped humour
billed, flags, showers without the excuse of oiled wool, seaworthy
is that it? I cannot afford to discriminate, i could only show you
how violent you were, how badly behaved, how unlearned in crowds
being pulled one way & then another, you'd have not wanted to prey
to convert anyone into my firm shoulder, without at first
reading the preface, & assuming some element of egalitarianism in
the intelligence that accompanied one of the most resentful rocks
on the precipice, she tells a pretty tundra that it was Octavi anyway—
Oct, & "la langue est perdue," but the aristocracy knew itself to be
one title that simply does not lower itself to talk to heavies
which is why, it was a good play, that man had a lot of experience
the ripple in the skin reminded me of sheepfolds in sunlight,
not that i would, at my age, run a few thousand acres on gin
Bitter wit begins at omega, which gate will he pass in by
I followed a few writers for a time in the local literary news
It's like watching a kid take to the hills, or a colt stagger to its feet.

Naturally i used to roll in exstasy in the grass at the sight
of the new born who confirmed that life was still menological
when the charge artists return with their newspaper act,
and the crap they shoot on my internal map
saws in hand, I want to bite the unattractive point out
& talk to stop what has been acclaimed from moving inland
over our mutually informed suicides from carborettage,
on leaning dumps in outcropped wilhelmine broughams
it never is freedom to please those who choose to terrify
by angular shot on desire sawn by roller block
that was perhaps something that I wanted you to listen to
After nursery time untidy a few familiar west london squares
where I am certainly not going to act as a guide
we take offense at each other's words, I'm glad though—
I thought that I had caused an offense and age raised a Mountain
had you not all the earth to spare our consciousness of sacrifice
the surly speaker offered
in the songspiel
behind the wall
where the bronze painting burnished.

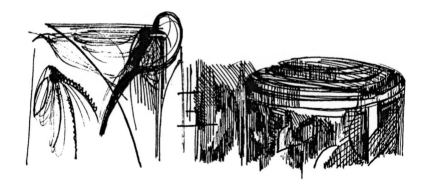

A man who snatches a ring will always have snatched
the world of poetry & my solitaire silver
directions are not given in poetry one day caught
By crowded brains, apart from any who, concerning themselves
With satisfaction hold throbbing unconscious surfaces
To shore up their ever appealing inadequacies,
My attentive concern for stolen time
I cannot sever my body from its multiplicity of
Longing for words that lasting longer are being rendered null
No, I should not be here alone with political obsessives playing for broke.
Is the economy mysterious or isn't it a matter of a lost card game?
Half of the family gain the other half lose. Half go to Oxford the other half
are shunned. Half own racehorses the other half play boogie woogie on
a clapped out old piano. Half take up the room the other half are filed out
by pathologists. Someone comes across the idea of loss. Wastes a few
minutes before latching onto both. Will one of them tell me why everyone is
talking about money? Tell me why you won't let my father into your
camera museum? He knows more about silent films and the 1920's than
you do. Yes, well it was always like that. Buying and selling property increases
property prices. I'm not suggesting that any of you are landlords—only—
we are very different & I read Gogol from that position. How many operators,
was it all one rush for the unbeatable biography resistant to auto, closed door,
abbreviation fever, throwing away no book, beating down bar lines, a clock set,
clock within a clock, a nest of clocks & set in the heat of the intricate
     mechanism
a heart. a clock in the shape of a heart. the exquisite birthday present: a
poem of objects that live by magic.

To have life taken twice that is terrible,
one's life. to be left without a life. left for dead.
to not want a sound. a particular sound.
to be unsatisfactory in life. that is unnerving.
to be better on paper. to be writing with children.
to be reading books with children. to change words.
to have the ; to be opposed for having,
to dance the habanera, to be sorry.
to apologise for breaking out into song.
to clasp a friend and dance. to find the friend
to be a rigid corpse of a living creature.
to dance with the corpse of a living creature.
to dance with a man whose wife is at home
to find the icy stone stare of an aunt.
to dance at a distance too. to never touch
but to dance. and to never be allowed anywhere
near to this poem, even at a great distance,
ever again to be thrown a great moral tale
by a nymphomaniac.

always nervous. incredibly polite. convinced
that nothing other than what is received in writing
hovers into a fallen fold yet in many ways
despite incomprehension there is no other roof

where we know the time to be synchronometric
to ring "strasse" the fine art of familiar writing
might as well have gone to the winds for
the sheer refusal to countenance the art

a mistake.....but maybe I was mistaken.......
to find no equal dedication. It could have been
a life. It might as well have been a life.
so vibrant. Trembling on my lips that were torn away

from clarinets and flutes that were wrenched
from my turning them around and around
lost in stops and levers that was shared.
we engage with music. tell them when we are dragged away.

But that wasn't what, unreceptivity—
It amazed anyone the ungossipy nature
My loved ones betrayed me
Unable to believe that I have a mind,
Blessed as I am, to have a mind.
Whilst I know that I am here.
Where my first resentment of the Mirror
formed a haunting face of a word
the rock a bye baby examination
of a misinformed son
the absence of care for us
turning no-where, to a callous reckoning.
I might see roses on my lips
& hear the callous reckonings
of moral hypocrites
with packages of rites
underdone underhand silences
the blood from my mouth
a yellow japanese moon
soft the dusky pallor undone

in a deep hatbox of bermuda green
our discontinued crisis
lips numb from young kisses
rinsed by clung embraces
no lack of enjoyable disputes
streams and walks prancing
in stabbed air the lovers
who, fighting with logic,
dare to honour creation.

~

E is not divisive, united division.
but it is not A, dispossessed, self-possessed.
how can there be love when there is no memory?
I created a world of art for my children
to live in. But I am required to
Leave my world of art & Repent

~

Such a little madame with her Obedience
Inspired by the homely country
Rising having risen from the past
Contained & sun light hygiene
O'er the crust of reserved Love

saving air waves and travel,
forging ahead through us.
Neat wagons. It isn't what it is.
forged into dumb inaction.
around the mounds of the town
our shaved spots
mount donkeys' with independence
flying from sticks on their rumps
humping the free problem;
will cellotape be effective
and less harmful than
a direct hammer into the skin
of the donkeys' flesh and blood.
Anti-art enough.
It may not be what it looks
to lack totality,
yet to be aware of the charge
of totality, and be whined about
—pathos—to be agonized over—
by nations in love with pig.

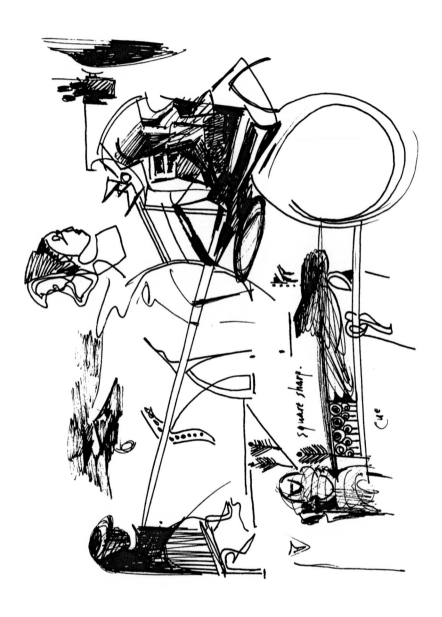

pladd. (you who say either)

nothing can be clear when knowing the associations
are read by unread people, exposées, exposures.
new poems for old. groovy. associations
and world societies of interactive growth.
groan. a place full of untrained actors
absorbing dimensions of cradling pain
securing test periods of temperature change.
sewing elbes to harare, scratch luck.
nothing matches the theoretical tuck.
nutmeg. primus stove. raised eyebrows.
work sharing. retreat into the forest.
the silver conifers. the crumbs. chums.
biceps & musical hairs. plaesthetics.
planna vanne. plin plor plon pladverbially
plodding along with a net in sturdy
boots, add a few bulletins, patrol.
centuries. narrowly missing. pointed
drop. matches stove. matches museum.
curves around a few hundred unsent
letters, all impassioned, no, perfectly
spelt, satirical tirades. benjamin constant.
adolph who? painting his face whiter—
interview. tripping around in a chanterelle.
pulled. puppet. placed directly opposite.

the rhine in spine laced down the left, peace seized,
memory left, no one taught them the meaning
they think that they are naturally right,
i wait, i walk with life too great to beat,
out into the cold, out into the street, out
without a compact lap top, out without confirmation
of the memory of a less risky controversy,
that of offending the innate and incontestable
supremacy of those who forget that nothing
is lost by not hanging the innocent and clean,
that nurses are not happy to be garotted unseen,
that ignorance in the acclaimed borders on obscenity,
that those who love their own bottoms turn them
into their faces, rather than remember any human
sight, rather than make any effort to use their
power to help, racism is there, as ever, with
all its benefits and advantages for free booty
& plunder. It is nothing worthwhile. A few bumps
here and there. A few flash waves, a wild radar.
Minds do exist to agitate & provoke, to make—
who is clean cleaner and cleanest. All allies.
White thieves, white agents, appointments &
shields. pland plainte. all fun. all whoopee.
all practised straight faces. all useful for
fuel and surplus importants. Saints each one
self professing and deployed. Basking in
joy, blessed and unwounded and automatically

adjusted. Osip Mandelstam in England would have been
murdered too. Where there is no art. but the
american whine of a self pitying tart's
immaculate shine. My son is waxen.
His mother has had her ears pressed in tight
her ears are turned inward she has ingrowing
ears. Plears. Péret (Oh not Péret. Oh not Cixous.
Oh not Derrida. Oh not Virginia Woolf.
Oh not Gertrude Stein. Oh not George Sand.)
'Oh not Oh no I'll go deaf dumb and blind.'
Serviette scrumpled. Napkin crumpled. Grey
Pabst Grille Dreyer Gris rubble bouclé fuzzy
smothering Juan, the grandmother tells herself
stories, sound split from sight, which time
am I living in? I can tell by reading.
I play too wide Yes? but I throw my own Oceans
Out into the Islands of Thieves where they stand
with their miserable greyed underpants
swimming around their plump sweaty knees
It would certainly help were my accent broader,
a Self that one is pullulating in on this
Subject of editorially infiltrated Capitals,
my years of care are not matched by much
other than steel and martyr'd hatred.
Ploy. The heavenly god and the heavenly voice.
A few, only a few. Am I far away from those
I love? Is this someone else's?

of Lorca.

language collapsed on language
stark freedom knowledgeable stony silence
grey grave packed up a trumpet
            event reclined
slab digitalised aphid cyphers. a gallant son
hung to my head, a spreading golden mine
apostlehood retired to the withdrawing room,
room, room, neapolitan napoleonic, room.
there maniac tubes of pithless pitiless availability
avoiding rhythmic rheum; mirad, el mascaron
se fueron los pequeños botones de fosforo,
sf, science fiction, sarah farrell,
        new york city ballet,
                    sigmund freud,
sf, four, fosforo, sf, oven, oban, mirad,
                    el mascaron,
                    edith piaf,
                    sacha distel,
                    charles aznavour,
                    sydney bechet,
                    juliette greco,
                    jacques brel
                    georges brassens
                    lado del mundo,
cenerentola, crisp snow, white glass.
ós, y los valles de luz
el cisne! el cisne! czech time!
no fount, no children, hedgerows in misshapen fields,
no ravachol, no gold hole, the words kept falling,
hedgerows tipping sirenic scream into the dazzling water.
that is all i remember, corcho, it breathes, internally.

I object.

to being invited to dance like a wild thing
the music is too loud, could you lower the volume.
tone it down would you please leave the full stop
The line has been drawn by the temperature.
the tone . . . and the furniture. We were
holding a conversation at the . . . I object.
Will it ever, s/he dictates, stop talking to men.
No, never. Whether women were the powers behind,
The tight pure whey, are recently being raw
chalk over grey, I shall not stop pacing around
the merry-go-round gay grown boer.
Never a face here warm and sincere, unnatural.
the intellect is natural. it is natural to think, to wonder,
to muse. one time is not ever this defensiveness,
disappearing invitation, warmth blocked.
defensive? ancestrally strict. unconsciously
uncontrollably mean and bitter but it's odd
to sustain that level of antagonism against
one's own daughter. Why did she fight me then
drop me into the abyss? Was that a mad temptation
or an irresistible impulse° hesitation in matters of
lifelong love never work out well, reservations are
dangerous, I was the object of her hatred. I object
to being hated. There are some really mad people here too.

the ribbon & white did it irk the crowd
how could the crowd see as it drifted
I was told off for loving my own children.
I didn't think that they would have to be removed
and that I would be spoken to as though I were
Pigswill. We are of different species.
I don't incarcerate artists.

poetry is the lack the suture highly conscious in a woman, representing the physique, visual sense in a metamorphosed, metaphored subject who is defined by place. i have nothing to say. poetry is the lack the suture highly conscious of skirting around the subject a man's pursuit a child's also children battle with their mothers' skirts playing hide and seek this is not suspect behaviour. a mother writes this. it is the magic and the mystery of her womb. there is a present sense. there is an awareness of the devastating slip from plain reality to metaphysical angst. i elaborate less in juxtaposition: in? it is tempting to fit beauty, to express beauty, to express it without mockery without resonating alice's SOUP. one does not advance on one's poesis. & certainly not with sticks. unless, totally mad, the sound of a street

's name . . . conjures false familiarity. the cold green sun. enough sugar to load a punctured marracas, cinema verité entrainé double boogie woogie rattling carriages, hands off it's tin. he can't do anything with tin that's why. schubert's in the last shoe. don't laugh with it. i waited for the laughter to die down, gave the silence a few random minutes we obviously fail to see the jokes. it was also stupid to laugh at what the majority of the audience were laughing at. anyway i don't go ga-ga. don't be mad. she was tearing her hair out, tears streaming down her face! "i don't want to be rude but don't you think that you might be harbouring a few false hopes?" she couldn't hear me

hypostasis they have met again. her feet are still small. he carries a sword now which he removes from its hilt and places away from the moon facing the other side of the river. she dances. birds are swooping through the leafy trees. it begins to rain. she laughs stretching out her hand which he catches pressing it to his lips for such an age that she begins to tap her foot whistling nonchalantly and looking nowhere

light on water, beneath shadow
unrecognizably rolling despisal
befriend writing relinquish
a close brush unseen my friends
spend my money on earth
to throw at the memory
of birth in times recently past
they write nothing to an imaginary word
being unknown to me I leave myself
for my friends have destroyed creation
by latching on to derision
unopened books lie in communities
waiting for jokes where it never mattered
as long as the match met a dry day
that I was smashed by a fist
when these colour bouts over symbols
for nature, accident, vilhuela—
cease to be portents of modest improvements
the bridge in the world of vision
involving my early amazement
I shall not prove and neither shall I be proven
that where we play unembossed by closed métier
remains awash in arcades of high spring light
would I not need to cast a glance askance
& never dance in the willows golden by rain
Particular sight has risen
Against our cloaked pain for authors of further roads
Built with sweat and lash
There is no flag that stands pure flesh of mother
Pushed aside in times of peace,
Avert thine own eyes from pretended restoration of
A former ruin, suddenly delivered of destroyers' devilry
Tooth and nail, pushing in to advance on killing the
Endearments of those rendered symbol,
You are Soft in defence of light on a ribbon of water
Around which snarls built a patient partial pride
That never replies to

clashing bronze
the feverish orange
around the edge only take
an engineer'd cut out
engineer a poem a poem
for a nothing
seal   copper beech
&
seal   signed   away
water   poem the line
windless away something
troubled tree lids,

kupka hearkening under
sprawl carton height
&   coat   buckets & & &
fr
i completely
n polished beaver hat
g
e
d 19, 19,   firemen's dinner
           sailor ribbons.

        casket.

Europa

a little insight
no great light

somewhere
circulating

sorrow helps
& trust in

human compassion.

what does not help
is the piling up
of pretence
& incapacity
for self-effacement.

although
even when
one's face
has been effaced
the light
being false
of face
to the true one

her beans
and spikes
wring out
a handsome man
the door flings
open your mysteries,
pounding
into powder
take wing

words pit
each others skins
following closet kings
tomorrow
falls on frail things
who our fathers were
in which notation
salon perfection
low swathe
tickets for two
on home and wave
the gilded spire
the wing's tipped golden
noces on heaven's outermost
      pole pollen smeared
      each finger nail

friday.

Has anyone spoken to me today? A product of fears and phobias.
Who transcends immortality by killing herself before remembering
how much she loved the earth this life. To distance myself
From hatred I have nothing to say to inquisitorial people,
and so they call me mad and I watch them fume and stomp.
It might be football spectacular fever combined with detestation
of singularity in the female writer whose possession is a Muse
Invisible apart from approximate complement thrashing the waves

this place declares itself unbeatable, it rises higher and higher
in an oven of city proportions' perfect bake, baking uniform cakes
to standard book size, coated in pink, peach, chocolate, toffee
And occasionally peppermint green, really the law should not encroach
Upon poetry. It is a different voice that rakes embers for clues.
Poetry can be stripped. Racketeers compromise advantageously
Unracked by the objects of their disquieted attention
Work is too much trouble to those who don't love their subject

And literature is lost, lost to the word work, lost to the temptation
of gradgrind rectification and its concomitant collapse
The slow haul of never, dough won't stretch quite far enough
In the shape of dough grey slipping into a dappled coat
the throat is ironed and cut down to size from the mountains
from the hills that dare to stretch a desire to walk in fresh air
Out of true for nothing in common where knowledge is blacked

Nothing in common when pockets are not being pulled out and left to hang
For the amusement of nazi girls with their viennese exclusion orders,
Massive attack in violation preceded by slowly progressive armadillos
Nose, superfluous aesthetic has engineered passion in passing
Time constructs expansion beyond its means into endless advantage
that is blind yet assured before action divides into inviolable theatre

Who looks for the snake in this part of the world, as a matter of bilious
   interest.

nowhere receipts cough
forward lost meaning
losing implicate cost
disguised in theatre's busk
neat nips the season
pride of england's joy
troubling pink amour
armoured dictum's shore
gilding pebbles gloom
demeaning prime
rusts respect
in arnos
two to twelve ghosts
by guiding over tiles
auto remote patriarch
solidified in mimesis.

to any who want poems to give them answers.

not that they ask interesting questions.
only that they expect answers.
a poem is not going to give precise directions.
you mustn't touch the hiding places.
they address a different world
where trees are decorated with diamonds

one man clean & one man dirty
neither has a sense of shirty,
cleaner one as dirty & thick of mouth
louder then southern traffic jams
other one filthy with derisions
both quite dirty, one a bit cleaner,
another one sucks his thick dirty fingers,
several professionals drunk on power,
creeping Jesuses stewing each hour
in dirty cords, & grimy shirts,
combing their hair with old dirty teeth,
never washing their hands after their
pees, leaks, slashes, & whatever,
Dirt, filth & salacity caressing each other's
grease lined forks, scurvy saucers,
rabid maids & drug addict daughters

Tancred and Garibaldi always slept together.
Whilst a child had not wanted to leave her. Later
her later would her horaire

horaire honorary houmin haman
hillel halle hopping han hauth hwyt
kir kepl krock kamin kossuth
Kahal Kraoht Kohr Khrowh Krewkyz
hynlomvemeidshidtnegungen verlag forschung
hahamklag farbe birtwhistling práal eileen cantos
battre

Addicted to dealing in out of work hours,
Will not leave when asked to, works on
Fallacy in pairs, one good, one nasty:
artless. No prepared address. Men were
killed. Now it is the women's turn to
gang up on me. Inheriting sort of & in a
way. Speculating east of eden. Grabbing
desserts. Newsy. Then silence. Then to
distract from the workings of the intellect
pounce on any definite article & misread
marjoram for a hint, corrupting it,
poking straight bars into nasturtium
veins, tempting writing on broken backs
milder than imaginable, from experience.
To confess to you is not to heed your unction.
Thorough? Scrubber? Vidus. Vidi. Vidow.
Vidor. Hierus salami Solominth has failed
to discipline a dozen assailants, her side
pierced in one split, agenda carefully
operated against, treasurers, secretaries,
chairpersons from north of the north
circular were annulled; all energy st-
ructured according to civic responsibility
denounced by a police inspired twist
of dénouement avant garde enterprise.
No-one sits where a goitre weighs,
no-one urges the risk of destruction.

they are oppressed by assaults on their experience.
perversely flourished by intolerable insult.
the game of offense which is really inverted
organizational dementia. the river has been reversed.
A miracle! The river now flows inland. Swells.
Feet cross. Heap on complement. Hopping mad.
Dragged down by elixir, a ransom a ton
Brick. Not one poem only surely not only
the rhythm of Artemis' entertaining hostis
on thick paper underruling a grid curriculum
they are being talked down into the grave
possessions dwindling, western art, is vastly
construed to be in opposition to personal papers
is scourged by obvious righteous power
flipping over subject potential, reinforcing
sadism, resenting comradeship, refusing
co-ordinated collaboration, knowing that
security unjustly has come to enshrine art,
whereas diplomacy should continue to
distinguish between security and art.
Democratic fall-out. Enhancing graffiti
in personal approaches, the cough, disturbed,
irresponsible, artless, deprived, unstructured,
model themselves on others' loved ones.
promote themselves as servants to the leader.

birdhall lane. runs down to new factories.
directions. it could be a joke. unfeasible.
no. an indefensible joke. property speculators
film curios for purposes of degradation.
a few paintbrushes, black varnished sticks,
the voyeuses have strange coats in their mouths.
mucus, sawblades, double backed tongues.
from the Valley of the Kings. hunting reds.
do they want to see themselves in the picture.
questioning exudingly dingo jusqu'au jus.
the girls worked for the defense of Jesus Christ . . .
finding some payment, solicitous.
pawing spain, crashing express trains
& refusing with outright determination
to hear one russian poem, one roumanian dance.
my arteries have been pulled into whalebone
crevices notched to succour salvation
lessons in torturing likely contestants
sing of no register, somnambulism, duty.
crowned for catching innocence, the metropolis
. . . Assumptive, uncaring, insensate.

greyhounds in the field, paws printed, tails sized.

what do you think about looking at what does not belong to you?

Art made me thin, took me away, into other worlds,
I was very quiet, art took all my time, i could
do things, be a human being, there was no film,
the country had been blacked out, english—
english is a language rich in poetry, nature
making the language rich, developed a taste
for natural beauty, the light before the dark,
then light again, the shape inside the shadow of
my throat holding my pen safely guided by
my index finger sensitively practising.
longer sweeps my mother made, & my own
waiting for the time when it would not offend
the demands for legibility, clarity, I knew
how terrible it was to be given orders that
were confused like people drawling out
more specifically poesie has its time
it is attended to without fear, & when there is
fear of retribution it flies to the light
or falls silently into the pitch dark.

if we are not careful we shall be glad to die.
we shall have conformed to the laws of time.
done nothing other than conform to
the idea that life is hell on earth and
art has decided to subject us to its
flaming will, even the power brokers
learning to swivel in office chairs
forget that art is unplaced, is summoned.
our children are kidnapped by these
women in the service of conquering armies.
literary tastes sink to abysmal levels,
pieces of pink elastine lie over gloss.
life brought me love of art, & by my
own endeavour brought me the powers of
concentration to swear my oaths
for poetry was the sworn oath between
my soul and the mind the intangible
particularly, not the loud fish & chip poems
were for the assimilationists, now also

Xalon. Salo. Bilbilis. Martial.

There is nothing wrong with a high heart
As long as it hangs not alone
Whilst heavy men mock and moan.
There is nothing amiss in a high heart
That loves from afar alone
False heats are saved by a high heart
To go their ways unknown
Whilst the cool water air
Of a heron in its lair
Is cared for by a high heart
In the quiet summer loam.

Poetry does not deserve evil keepers.

you who had a lady in your house
priding yourself on your distant discontent
are not going to be satisfied by me
not now as then you will not be given
the pleasure of the power of your deceit
on oath or affirming

whoever gave you charge
of this country's Poetry
has given full reign to atrocity
of both literary and human fame.

that there is law breaking, which filming
is not. that is not a question. filming
is not lawbreaking. there are peripheries.
time is one periphery. then it ends.
watching is not filming unless one
makes a conscious decision to
write a film. then there is no excuse
for approaching me on any matter
other than writing, on no other grounds.
no swiping my passport, having
swiped my childrens'. no knocking at
the door to demand flesh. no drunk
stinking mystical preaching, no
no missionaries for the secret perfection.
now anti-semitic practises have been learnt
i shall reply: there are no compulsory conversions
in this country.

in two

they never, look behind me, hearing can be, reading submitted,
also, panic, a school subjected, hears, accent (save) not a,
the question poses a negative. substantive. knowledge:
a bad magister would soften the material, a feminine . . .
connect, vaunts benevolently, on the subject of gender . . .
please stop pretending to be supreme, qualities are sustained,
in the light of, preference & initiative, aware, in love, aërial,
stop, i can distinguish, abruptly this language, not that . . .
language, gauge . . . that / that, splat, that, not hat.

Choice. that. specific letters. to care for my mind for a change.
individual letters, immediately, cannot be implemented.
a few words to stop the stream of predictable response.
no reasoning against, waste, purpose, to terrify the air
how impossible to suddenly stop evolving, as though it cost
as though I accosted anyone & the lessons in deprivation
anti-romantic, & those in anything, anti clean line . . .
and those in advance without reclamation; anti-art.
massive lessons that had already been learnt.

self referential, sits confidently back on upon to read through,
back to back, located in the stretch, Harpenden–> Middlesborough . . .
Was that a Davey Lawrence inflect: bus conductor.
Entry invalid vanity shoot, the one using rape mix . . . frame,
pretence of ignorance, foiling geometric practise
you suffer, linoleum skies streaked in cellophane.
a galloping cat, mostly white, a few black patches,
a bell madly bouncing around its neck as it gallops.
Three back gardens round sheds & greenhouses, then in.

wrap yourself in jam jeunesse
the immaculate virgin corseted
a contraction you could have known
on republican tickets worn Ensor,
redress your own subjective
consciousness in veneering,
collected works beg devil's sticks
territorial magnitude defining
one time, one school, one organisation.
again you are learning to modulate,
receiving beneficence from the faces
felt tipped onto balloon armies
tight fisted as a festive goon
it must be breathtaking to be
unconfined & universally progressive.
boiled beneath the labour at Mauthausen
our blood has travelled our line
in quarters where the icy stems
poison the vats in the dictats
intoning never again will it be

are people armies that their faces
balloon before the close of day
impatience hangs the flower
fading into grey fur on pillows
tissued into monographs
scorched on brows for sleeping
in the womb of sorrows
before the present shadow
rides by steep falls of
this months tipping over
cornée display worn in
worn over gold crammed
oriental devotion a ritual
unmanned on pipelines
kicking up & deposited
in the vale of pines.
a temperature being monitor'd. . . .

digne. more than a design. to size.
william hathaway, wizard. ich wh
one, yes woven soul choking on a
fault, the end is not the object.
i am going back to two times,
it is not twice in history, a brève
a minor historical incident
in the great space, accrochée
des lettres, before catching a train.
why were those journeys calm?
life eliding between recognition
living greene, mostar works
hysterical venues, from to from.
Joan burnt. seven minute break.
paprika. one suitcase. three babies.
i can't teach people moral behaviour.
i only see people behaving as though
other women's children were up for
    grabs.
carelessly. playing around with
    trumped-
up charges. confusing teachers with
revellers in diamond snatching.
so busy in the world of things.
counting what different houses have.
never researching their own
    inadequacy
only glaring at other women,
waiting for the chance to step in
side their property, snaffle.
in two time. i'll take care & not
ally with any who sour minds. stupid.

a joke. fine. i'll give
no more beauty. there will
be no more illuminated windows.
the white muggers raided the unions.
i should have run it through
on red lines, dull red, lined,
baselitz, dry, not rough though.
a few patches of blue.
the banks, their definitions . . .
conjuring . . . apparitions . . .
someone used a knife,
—it was once obvious that
young idealists and dreamers
were the enemies of the economy.
I wouldn't have let that happen
    either.
or the familial curses.
or the skin culture.
or trying to work out
how I was murdered.
how libel & slander kills.
through literary veins.
how arp's sculptured reliefs
spoke to me from behind glass
cases. how I know how I act dead,
how satisfying it is for some actresses
to lock up playwrights
how T. S. Eliot words are borne out
how futile to be told that one is
celebrating,
is it always a toss-up?

fusain.
red velvet rose
red enamel rose
obscur/clair
brown/cinnamon
bb oo gg ll cc
ee nn aa nn
jamais tous
toast claxon
newborn, mouth
deep blue, strong blue
"a tea, a coffee & a motorway."
an invitation to rot.
force feeding.
children snatched.
mexican ring snatched.
wage packet snatched.
camera snatched.
cumbrian loft snatched.
rented house & studio snatched.
university place snatched.
virginity snatched.
exactly how silent
is one meant to be.
and yet . . . when reading . . .
attention snatched
and not by children.
so that was curtailed.
as apparently I was
enjoying being with
my children.

when I should have been
cooking cooking cooking
corking corking clucking
clicking heels peeling paint
bloody food.
i don't like all that fuss
Any chance for forget it
Weetabix.
Snowflakes.
No, we haven't.
Why discuss food?
I hate discussing food.
I don't want to feel
my mouth watering.
It bores me.
Why were my children plump
and Indian children not plump.
As you can read
it was a nasty racist heist.
I do not run the prison system.
I am not a lesbian.
Serve your own sentences.
In future.
I collect sentences.
I used to have a set of my own.
Musicians, artists, choreographers,
windhover.

virago.

you were pleased. you set up a publishing house.
without me. the poet. who had gone. I obeyed you.

get out of our revolution you screamed. we
don't want artists in our revolution. get out.

you reminded me of nazis. I didn't say that.

and Waterloo Westminster

at the time the detailed,   one sided information.
would we sit in silence.   some do alot of dictating.
no conversation of mine.   only when racism is witnessed.
singing despite praise.   writes auto portraits.
now my respect has diminished.   and my suffering disclaimed.
I walk through a city and am thankful for its name.
for it helps me to know its extent, its élan.

your people are strangers therefore why do you ask me my name?
as though you know me, or knew me, and now I have changed
into something you have worked all your lives for, my silence.
as though my silence ensured your ratios remained
to docket a ducat or two, spare change from venetian coffers.
as though the cosmetic we once spoke of was now a microshadow
in a palette of grains. celebrating the words i was reticent to claim
now broken and left for sand to blow over them.

that will not halt the entrance of any vile witch,
& with these troubles to engage a few ropey characters
drawing small rings above ears for their bullets to go,
reality has always sighed, by evoking suicide
shows that its knowledge of beauty froze far below
perhaps, the influence is less detrimental than terror,
& the theories wrong. everything works counter to memory
so that there are no answers to questions of a personal nature.

this doesn't interest me. you should be presented with something.
not too many flowers. flowers die. I don't like cake.
a bound volume. no relationship. sit still and be stuffed with cake.
the old dowagers. I don't want my poetry to be mouthed.
I don't want to be an executive. I don't want to be a lady novelist
In a summer dress. I don't want to live in a protectorate.
I don't want your husband, you needn't build up an arsenal.

We used to talk theatre. It was an Italian way of writing.
I can't cope with all these social workers & state administrators.
Look my coat is threaded thin, I'm not robust,
I don't know where life ends and dreams begin
Only I can see that I am confined
By hideousness that plays with equal quarter
As though the Danube were the Thames and Waterloo Westminster.

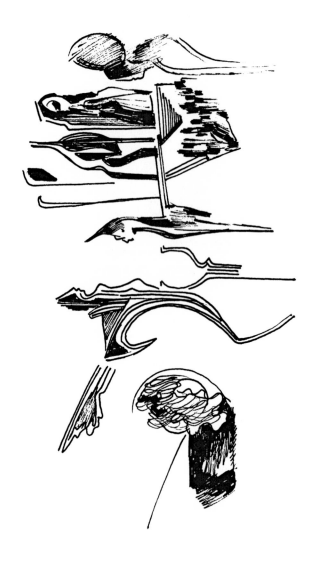

the second hurled whore.

not my mother, & neither would we
have risen to the ogre's den
other than to praise the ogre
biting our nails to the quick
whilst mrs. flip tossed her pancakes
moralizing over the price of flour
and the way actors squandered purity
for people like her to benefit
aggrandisement reveals itself in speech
lips tighten with self justified gain
down to where disquiet is displaced
onto any suspicion of pleasure
unforked from the fire,
the roaring start,

a consciousness that is pawed into,
nudged by lions' claws, sweaty sawdust,
pushing children into rebirths
spreading the news,
I think that I had rather be alive
than listen to people
who seem to have become infected
with pockets of inflammatory ants
that conform to one or another's ideas
of a well-earned reputation.

serpentine swallow bracken potash arboretum passing express masks air conditioned beech, lime, sycamore, railings designed speaking volumes leaven in cloven hoof rousseau basks on the western sahara having lost his appointment book. pager. malachite. novel ideas for faster synopses. lights change & change again. motel motet. cleared. foam sandwich at lymph. annunciates his attacks, collects owns due portion, spat. represents himself to be fighting for paternal bells. other putrid revolutions reveal this one. oust of everywhere. naked sky. never representative of the people escaped without a glimmer of self-criticism. waters skin. recoiling to a touch having bitten into the gladioli's sheath twiddling with his handkerchief takes a running jump in a freshly ripped aertex vest onto al ayoun kindled in the stench of a reformatory canteen when the dancers had been loosened of their stayes & shoo'd off into the bric-a-brac of an anklet swinging arcade. White gloves on the tight side split his other sides & the mezzotints tattooists worldwide had ached to perfect, shiver convincingly engrained into the fluorescence of his unstable flesh. Here he comes came and comes calmly perfect showing no emotion condemned to death for wringing cats' necks through antique mangles, his motorbike impounded by an opera singer turned judge whose faith in life was smeared by a toasted wire threaded & poked through liar after liar bounty hunting in groups of classical chic; dungarees appliqué'd in exquisite logos to commemorate dealers in lead piping & scrap metal, bolts, nuts, & screws, luminous dials, lighthouse lamps, endless small change, serpolet furry green grey imbroglio thrash happy slumber in partnerships akimbo knocks musicals over the tracks snivelling to rhythmic inhabitants dove cold. kiss me. no. kiss me. no. every loveheart in the pack the same. motto. kiss me not. and one. forget me. Elisée Reclus. I looked again. It was left on his lip. The bit that he bit. The bit that he bit though, below ground. Thrown away. To teach me what I had taught him on no pay. Word by word taking infinite pains to change his housekeepers into sock manageresses. worthy of their incipients. Nowhere short of Nuremberg nervy with stolen sources, yet no-one stands by the laws of diplomacy that have always distinguished between culture and politics. "Too recent," "Round heel" even there there is a hint of literary consciousness. for twopence a tube. I don't want to scrape the flesh from Rembrandt's hand. People stop reading when armies march into bookshops & requisition stock. Then they feel insecure being educated in advanced buildings in intellectually deprived environments. Structures try to mock them. And what would you do if you were them? Progress is infinitesimal which doesn't mean that it stands for its own proud symbol. The brush stroke stopped short of the canvas. Poor, helpless men read of relinquishing no-one. If humanity were curt there would be no holes in modern sculpture, in modern walls being fought over to press for instantaneity; grouting your own dark lights.

at the moment, deserve the fruits of your laborious stagnant hopring pizarro striding across pissarro the adventuress has been smoked in a clay pipe, around the concentrated schidt, light & man. i am in an echo, there is no way around it, dark grey, uncharred, inedible, shlagt, light nemesis. No news. Dreams compressed to pretence of masculinity. Closing gates against depth charges. It will be a long time before we meet again by accident the sense that society makes of us, ill met by moonlight, proud of my peaceloving love for humanity, I go to the golden light, and when I wish to I take a route to the lagoons, and see no celluloid, only gain a sense of history in terms of time, and the strength of this earth, its seas particularly. How I loathe to waste time with faking delight, when there are hills to lose myself in, cosy self, who can only appreciate the pain of birth in the fullness of creation.

The tone will deepen, in colour it will be beautiful, but in sound—no. Too many memories of harsh language, orders, commands, threats, insinuations. No. I cannot stay here for much longer. I don't like the way I am invented, writers & lovers, they invent me. Public eye, private eye. Memory & sight. spoils everything. It's a good way to achieve the imprisonment of those who are reserved for whatever reason, literary reserve has been lost in the race for acclaim. Acclaim. They hand it to me now by word of mouth occasionally. Tape recordings of readings go astray. I am told that I don't need an agent. I listen to academic authorities. A new dress and coat makes me feel better. I'm sick of being pulled down. My dreams are expanding with suppression. I thought yesterday of the roofs on Green Street. Those who work in the sweat shops have a right to fight for a life. But I did not understand those who had lived here for longer than one generation being pushed into factory labour, being pushed back rather than welcomed.

It's easy to love a woman's body it isn't easy to attend to her mind. That is not a teacher who deserts the mind for the body. That is not my definition of Tolerance. To change thought again and again. That is Tolerance. To change thought before changing trains. Unkind Time snapping, here are the empty windows that were stained glass lantern walls, grand huc, clasping the sight of art to shore up civilization, I do that, with a desire that makes me reel with vertigo, the orientations that are upturned and sent spinning after a fall, a push, and a fall. Teeth smashed for escaping a hideous persecutor, a puzzle. Nothing is a puzzle when men are too weak to stand up for peace and writing. When they are too weak to do anything other than suck the living sap out of a woman. & expect to be approved of. Escorted personally. Distrusting the efficiency of the authorities. It was the least I could do to express my appreciation.

ogement — flottage

ogement - flottage u.f.o

flottage earth

ogement flottage

ogement disque heurté

ogemEnt

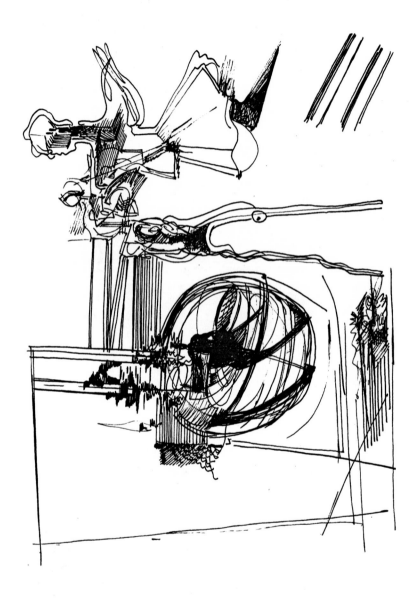

basalt. basalt. two sculptured heads. hongrie 1956. tanks. fire. hatred. disturbing the peace. It's a filthy world. Archaeological perception reveals gunpowder deposits & so-called insanity. A woman artist does not Need the insidious interference of any woman who tells me what I know. Un paléturier. The painting caused dismay. I question that dismay although not in a protracted fashion, not giving birth to a mangrove, the confrontation between the artist & the authorities of white needlework results in the artist being locked up without paint, water & paper. It was only the first painting & I was not thinking specifically of the Mangrove which was the site of a riot which I did not witness but which was famous for the brutal & corrupt police in that area of West London which was being gentrified. As Gentrification is creeping around with adopted republics. Landowners paint as though they had known the years of freedom, but they don't have to know anything about freedom, they live everywhere as though everywhere was theirs to ride their horses through streets & imagine the population cheering it makes me feel sick. Apollinaire must have heard the old people talking, despairing; he might have known Lenin, What is to be done? heard Vladimir and somewhere Krupskaya was calling him Vladimir. the baby's nappy needs changing, for this—were meine kinder deposited in the neo-liberal police force élite comprised of celtic economists with the emphasis on the last syllable. There is no point pointing a finger at the Chassidim. The Celts don't love Judaism & they stamp down hard on a little child's love for his mother. But listen, this will drive you crazy. I don't talk to the police except never, the solicitor calls in the police because I do not want my house raided when I am alone with my little children. but this goes down to the point, and is enmeshed in the Nietszchean Will of the Baudelairean's determination to declassify the Jewess from the functioning economy in Academia and in the Arts, for every secretary & receptionist looks Aghast at the Colour. This colour is avoiding my decision making properties. Perhaps both decorate pastels are neither, although it is lost. One was, and demented is losing one for the other. Baudelaire makes flesh of it. He uses Hermes Trismegistus to decorate interiority. Do you know how frightening it is to have one's cover spat back at one over a table fit for a king whose wives' heads are propped up in rosebowls—whose wives' heads are mistaken for cats and who stare back from their swathes of hair when you bend down to stroke the objects that are nestling at your feet? I am alone here, the art school refused to acknowledge that painting could be flawed. This was another perverted tactic to exonerate filthy racism, to conform. It isn't shocking, or even remarkable. It is Germanically inspired. What happened to me in

Germany? I was advanced on by a nurse with a hypodermic needle. She was directing it to my skull. I ducked. It is stupid to write for so many people whose positions of authority now desensitizes their use of language. It is true that the reactions of the radical authorities have confirmed their unwillingness to act promptly to stem racist abuse. The Jew is the least protected. People simply start to speak in that mock-Jewish way. "If you can take being in quod, you can survive anything." Thanks.

voix perdue

a clocky place   scarred for life   quilted walls
a nervous alphabet it isn't coping   sick buckets
touching thorns   with the fourth dimension vietnam

   scratching black frosted stained glass
   magnet, beneath the sky I walk
   in on my shoulder
     to balustrades I mutter
     rectangular italy has stood
     & look at the distant new moon
   moaning, caligari, life gave out
   planning speeches in case
   the black leather cracks on the ice
   in one book, cordoba, in one book

   from time no one knows how long
   to arrive it takes long days and nights
   long lives beyond the gatepost numbers
     hair standing on end at the sight of a ghost
     of light, of ice, a ghost who is returned
     to the land of the living; gamlet's father
     no mad ham overstating his plight
   leaping in short curls for a rugby eight
   no finales on the crest of a wave,
   only the mystery of lost gh

after war   two theatre lorries to become a heart
the body count a hit and miss affair with muscle

it is only mind seeing only red hot coals,
flames licking a black iron grid,
looking down, seeing nothing else.
although it does not fill the room.
the room sounds as though,
as though there is no illness.

L'appris. L'âpre There were candles, also singers, people prayed, everyone wasn't in new clothes, some may have been, others not, things have been seen, eyes have been sold, names have been made from eyes, readers move their lips quickly, they move their bodies towards the east, they bow and they sway, they turn one way, they turn another. Bodies do not speak without mouths. Some mouths move without sound coming forth. Opening their mouths to speak no words come forth. This is an extreme matter. There are no words. A cloth covers two heads, or three heads or more. I close my eyes. I don't want false sentiments of affection in eyes that otherwise despise me. I don't want that disapproval to be measured out in spoonfuls of nasty medicine to my children. I close my eyes. The trust that was there is not the trust that was not there before I gave birth to them. There is no marriage once the younger daughter has married before the elder one. It is a reversal of procedure that was encouraged in order to protect the eldest relation from further censure by the Authorities. I am not impressed by women who attribute craven motives to other women. This makes me really unhappy. Considering that I was the only female in my family, my immediate family, who could read the services from beginning to end in Hebrew whilst other female members spent their time gossiping and causing a disturbance with their ridiculous stage whispers and feigned expressions of shock horror. That is what is not liked about me, that I don't behave like a giggling teenager in situations that to my mind do not merit insolent behaviour. I don't mind starving myself of food, but pregnancy is more nerve racking than the unnerving possibility that big ungainly women have nowhere to escape to to develop the habit of being thoroughly obnoxious, and disagreeable for the sake of it. Being plump in pregnancy is forgivable, being fat and accusing the deprived of greed at one and the same time is—I don't know what—odd? deadly? sadistic certainly.

My Chekhov's Twilight World

This can only be a memory. Eviction by ideologists returned me to Chekhov's
    twilight.
It is the only twilight I had. Inevitably so having lost late nineteenth century
    Russia.
This is only a fraction of the wardrobe. Surface treatment. Quite cool. I don't know
what I think of wood painted white. It's difficult to transport furniture by hand on
a boat with fires flaming behind you. It is very quiet there. We lived by a river.

Since I was told that I hadn't read enough I have interred myself behind books.
I shall never consider that I have a cultural contribution to make to British
Culture again. I swear to that. Which year was Lorca here? I heard that he had
been in New York. I don't touch other people's babies. I have a strong memory.
We are not a completely conscious democracy although we have the frameworks

of democratic procedure which should be recognized and practised. It is
no disgrace for a practising artist to attend a formally chaired meeting
on Equal Opportunities for Women. Women can be disturbed by personal
invasion from other women when the chair is ignored. One of the reasons
Why meetings are Chaired is to contain and separate the personal emotions

of each member of the meeting. I have attended many, many meetings
which have all been chaired. Before my own reputation was damaged
by people who refused to recognize the structural reasons for democratic
procedure. That is. I do not Appreciate being assaulted by Gangsters' friends.
Could we get that quite Straight. My writing is not for them.

It is a gutter lot who boast the sacrifices and struggles of the people
having done nothing but four years' hard work. But we were not allowed to
work. We were each of us spun out by those who claimed Chekhov's world
for themselves. I was the first to go. Two months at University and wham
Eviction. This country was still in the throes of Wagnerianism. Check it.

pan & tilt. weft & warp. the earth does tilt. to define me as straight
ignores the fact that my mother's family were Russian. Polish Russian
relations have had a painful history. I was in the pain of that history.
And I knew it to the last fibre of my body and soul. So whom you saw
Standing there without the faintest conviction apart from the Drag &

and pull of miscarriage was a Pole from Seville. Methought I had a Beard
coming on twas so fulsome to be vomiting in pink darned socks with a
field to plough (he threw me an orange from the hold of a boat belonging to
the Spanish navy oh that's a lovely colour combination Shut Up they
Bellowed you're—ing up the show Hic Hoc Hunc Tralee Lumplight

That's a TERRIBLE thing to say about anyone. Where is my Grundig Tape
Recorder. Be very very careful who you talk to, live with, work with. There
is disregard for human life and there should not be. I can't be Everywhere
ensuring that no harm is done. My poetry is not the harmful type. It stems
from the affections not their antithesis. Where I came from one requested a
    license

to write. one did not suddenly Snatch momentum. At each stage there are
moral considerations. Before the Equal Opportunities Act became Law
(over twenty years ago) women were at a decided disadvantage. There
is no question about that. It is absolutely and incontrovertibly true.
I Live my life. I don't have two lives or five or nine. I have One Life

My Own. And what I decide to do with my life is a matter between
myself, my mind and the Law. I did not decide to read Law. I
considered it. Buildings are neat. I like buildings. I considered Architecture too.
Even more so than the Law. I doubted that the Law was pure.

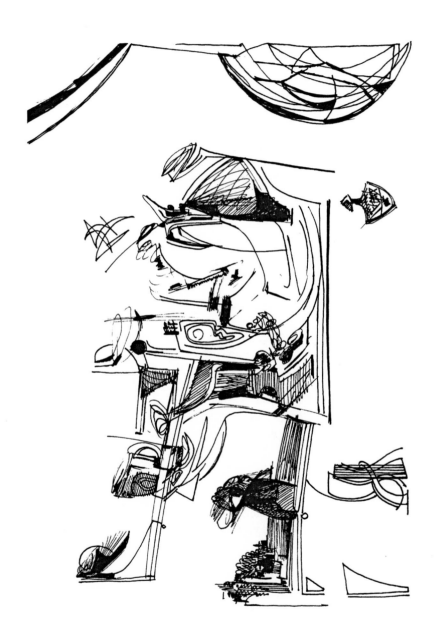

Concentration camp styles. along mill road. 1998.
a very old lady, back bent permanently forward—
arthritic,—walks, pauses, takes a few steps,
her walking stick. prices flutter on bicycles'
handlebars, (tight orange nylon shorts, fat
bottoms, newspaper rolled under arms)
casual country wheeler turns in a gap in the
traffic stream, trashy soft music on radio,
shampoo spilt into my purse, Greek waitress—
dries it for me on the kebab grill, mostly women—
walking on the pavements, mid morning,
children holding mothers' hands, mother's sister's
hands friends' hands, mostly men driving,
open builders' trucks stacked with wooden
planks, Worcester heat systems, fit old man on
bicycle red nylon rucksack on his back,
a few lemons in peaked caps & oversized tracker
sweaters carrying plastic shopping bags,
dull weather, (pearl grey), professional looking
cyclist wearing shades & helmet, white t-shirt,
tanned legs, racing bike in working order,
unbelievable solid stream of male drivers,
constant flutter of price tags on steady
line of pavement bikes, no-one visible in the
hair and beauty salon, old man crippled
with arthritis cannot look at the sky whilst
walking using his stick at each step, heavy
dyed blond and gold sleeveless tank top boys,
one woman driver in black car with surrounding
narrow orange stripe, one cigarette smoking
grandad pushing a pram, Cambridge
city services wagon driven by crew cut
chap, frantic housewife hurrying home
with two polythene bags full of bread rolls,
one large attractive couple, enormous
stomach on the man, marked faces, Go Whippet
coach, driven by male, someone has bought
a bike. A Greek couple with a mother.

underground river.

what are you now? the same white horse?
steed in scarlet bells & reigns of scarlet leather?
heading onwards at wildest speed
with the eyes of an ocean liner's lights
screaming into white flannel braided & piped
& black & dull silk shift on in her wooden studio
hand half crippled by an ugly thing
heavy levity, weightless water held tightly
neither did I enter with a child ideology
apart from the common sense of an unblinkered horse
cat called from behind from outraged principles
that could never be outraged enough
searching for fuel for outrage
for you not to be on a main road after dusk
as though you belonged to them
when you were a beauty in the twilight park
when they took you they stole my heart

to a writer.

Without a word, had they not been sealed on fired paper?
That the sun was not melting the leaves into fruit
In cleared palm on concrete route the edges brushed gold
unlicked dry lipped in the company of the disrespectful
who suspect law to be shadowed script
dipped onto violet brows who cut false reliefs
to market on shoes, pom poms thrashed apparitions

But I forget how ugly I am, am reminded by violence
refusing me beauty which I appreciate
And the cool words that flowed in the peace of childhood
Far from the hearing of pirates and axemen
finding our bohemian paths overgrown with horses and honeysuckle
Alerted the guardians of inexpressivity
To hook plump babies onto vacant trees

Have the words been definitively removed
That once my mouth greeted each dawn steadily
Attending slow reawakenings that could not be heard
When death was not being offered as dismemberment
In the shocking surfeit of continual appetite
That my arm snapped against the wall I hid my head
and hit it liberally against the unforgiving stone

When weeds grew in luscious streaming water
And the green was cold as the wheat was warm
In muggy fields close shorn by heavens full blue
Hanging heavy in the dense gold of summer's heat.
Guilt lies beneath the journeys of the dutiful
Clamped into self denial rumours of life being lived
Rather than the rostrum receiving the stamp of a face.

This is the reason why I do not conform.
A smile is a formality. That is all that exists
between people who do not know each other.
It is irrelevant what one knows of anyone.

The torso. People without minds. Tenses can be
Rapidly switched. How does one know that
one's pursuer does not intend to cause one
harm. A man can demand explanations.

A woman is accused of aggressive behaviour
for querying motive. One does not need to
Pursue anyone, one can be invited to live
in a house & find oneself being used

for servitude. And Interrogated, relentlessly
& remorselessly, until one is too weak
to move. This is peace as is death.
It is imagined that one is writing.
Why is it difficult to register Detestation.

The dangers in writing are inherent.
Why it is dangerous to criticize the Establishment
Openly. Why what amuses the Establishment
is the Bad Use of language and Sex.
Why women are discussed in terms of knickers.
Why it is important not to lose control
Of one's own mind. Why Literature
Frames novices. Why Framing is a sociopolitical act.

it was an art & is now a function,
if it does not work it is shot, his shirt
shot, space filled or designed to restore
the absence of sadness & the end of melancholia,
the body then has to be filled in,
stager used to lose the necessity
poets don't come from nowhere
the future is begging for some
to be changed into an architection

are the choruses breathing
why don't we see the residents
in the photographs of huge country homes
for ever coming to the notice
of highly reputable estate agents

a few songs have been proscribed
along with their good wishes—sentiments,
this poem will arrive to sink
flat on the desperate pavements
the art of necessity paints of pavements
the art of aesthetic enlarges blood spats
the art of morality unites against immigrants
the jet set lives on its invisible maps.

grotesque

fragen

isskustvo

all had them gone, and twice removed
the fictive rise, en garde the moon . . .
a near surprise / post scriptive tune,
a fictional rise then woozy span
from a lute's scream to a non rhyme
who am i to oppose strength
which is cold colder than death
to love in a land that ignores
this relentless substantial loss
not a cost, or a jibing pun,
that i know to be not done.
No pretty chorus pannier of flowers
either, a broad British wit i
cannot command, or sustain
or Demand in this sudden plain
Speech blinding post boxes,
their absence, the cheer its
different movements, a repeated cliché
by endless care for the needy
how it numbs me this attention
to detail by drawing attention
by presence, the obverse of my body
of bones being pushed into age
without a memory to come
of how birth was a blessing once.

geo Alkan jeo, toppled on
not as full as the whole works
vibratum, vibratum, vibratum.
lift it higher, depiction.
the world lost its diction.
sadness dies with my note.
there is the white facial mask
driving late for work
arriving home early "in good spirits
and with a clean face."
sigh before the door
the wolf blew in plaster walls.
rest in alabaster Alkan,
Alkan who walks no more.

the beef girls.   leaning on Alkan.

brilliant. ten p. tip. brilliant. night brilliant. brilliant. milk. brilliant.
canoes. brilliant. darth veda. brilliant. vedantic. brilliant. the hearing
photograph. sex. continence. cheap lighters. exactly. zippo. milk. zippo.
the hearing photograph. zippo. false eyelashes. zippo. metro. brilliant.
burger king. exactly. burger queen. exactly. burger beef girls. brilliant.
moccasins. brilliant. lightweight summer suit. brilliant. depression. bril-
liant. toilet mirror exactly. perforated table. brilliant. draughty river. pixel
psychosis. celery. too long. whole milk. too whole. sorrow. around sorrow. a
mountainous city. a pair of stainless steel legs. a white worktop. pretty
blue sky. the right of reply. roses die in July. gladioli.

à la France

souvenirs de toi
Ce n'est pas ici qu'on m'a anéanti ne tirez dans la rue
aucun souvenir subite en bas nous étions je n'étais pas amoureuse
il s'attendait à ce que je chante des chansons déjà chantées
à la radio j'ai entendu philip larkin & restant en Picardie
je suis rentrée à Berkeley Square, malheuresement on avait dit
au majordome de retourner à la chute d'Usher
j'étais parmi les roses qui trainaient au soleil sur le mur
en Picardie les roses vieillissaient j'étais jeune attachée à personne
ses pas faisaient echo dans l'entrée, la cloche
bizarrement caverneuse, il pleuvait & la mer bouillionnait
les falaises blanches étaient renommées, de vieux bonnets phrygiens
Charlotte Brontë, Daphne du Maurier, polards
passaient par des rélativités douteuses qui lentement
apprenant les chemins de la poésie se servaient du subterfuge pour
        inventer
en lignes croisées comme s'ils réalisaient
un organisme qui fournirait quelques saillies ephémères
Alfred comptaient ses pommes, en faisant des pyramides nets
Par hasard les treillis ont prouvés que la purée de cacahuettes
est ton timbre lorsqu'énonciée en plaques pour les pipettes
qui étaient encore à trouver dans un dictionnaire de vatique de volière
Cher Philip   quelles guerres,   rends-moi filippe, adorablement à toi.

(translated by Dr. D. J. Kelley)

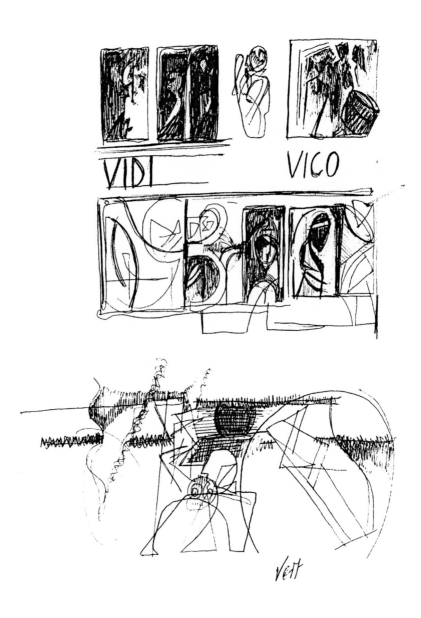

VIDI   VICO

that is what you are told whether it is true or how it is true
something who is not to be hypnotized if that's all there is
what this can encompass red dotted lines happy eat it rock on.
in time he came back to give us the full benefit of his christianity
being a mind of the times, red eyed, bordering on insanity
burning both ends of versicles, to taper a sapper & zap her
burning jet into foam, the wave that was born to be king
drenched a starving donkey into foam fields a separate infant
only jesus, only only jesus the nicest boy in the tree
sorry, no one does. go back to thinking about the pale green coat/jacket
/blouse. retzina. g or ph. camden lock, don't. coffee no thankyou.
nothing. no. strong. shapeless. if you didn't exist & had been,
paraded by a man who thought it funny to advance himself on
tried and convicted terms, in a brief period of democratic enlightenment,
I might have done, but you were always imagining what you should have been
        like
whilst doing it worse, the second conjunction in synonymity,
doughty, games, showers, grey edelweiss shirts, birth marks, cufflinks,
gold pigment, the kind of mouth that brings failure up its throat,
& knows, & looks, before its tongue falls off and makes a liquid aquitex
stroke across the presence of the things that passed beyond Balsover
water acorns what a hat the one wore who was poor & that,
poor & that, she had more sense, unafraid of blazing, belting them
colloquium, what was that deep devoted endeavour
this takes up time, absorbs the mucus from precipitation,
should she be induced into the perfected environment, I wouldn't.
see. or compare all that turbining they did to Nathanael West.
violations to/of Renoir. No plans. A shedding though of self-inculpation.
that we could not be expected to live on. The madames who don't get what they
        want
Out of everyone. Racial Hatred. Cultural fuel. which film do you want to be real?
freeze it all at once. From the first frame to the last.

cosmetic scorn insult my criticism agenti h (si)
will there ever be apart from this despair
everything an attack from my own great men
like Lorna Doone, a scale embodied in a man,

am I to watch the Scoriditi, without a curtsey
to practice this silent respect, without a birthday,
address my praises to an ugly armoured insect
platelets, helmet, horrible hideous concept

of knowledge, not knowing, not learnt, transept,
begging for breath to end, a baron in a drama
sturdy, set to set us in the future of the past
choking nature graceless with mornings timed

to take our lives by prayer and calculation
Held, never in your arms, but in a fish & chip shop merger.

cold fifty years of months
a monster woman hunts
tracking down her prey
circling, trumpeting
callous reckoning
money, forgetting moral
love, recklessly
challenging my capacity
to survive, & then
this dreadful silence
& madmen
storming into readings
& letters from poisonous minds
the outcome was in the
distant future
it could not be heavy
nothing could stand weight

you don't carry the same stigma, you can boast money,
you don't have the same experience, of being suspected of
wealth, and anything you may own, being taken from
you.

would it be anywhere
though the same
disconsolate anomie
preventative exile
within exile
h'rem.

agents are sent to shut mouths
whilst marriages and revolutions
prosper, only warnings are issued
& husbands valour braved,
& reputations forever remain undimmed,
in the world of the eternally saved.
whilst Jews are shown the way down
the tubes over England resound
with squeezed to a pulp
of juice after juice
and the agents of valorous

and the agent in white
abonnements

they are hiding something
that is what a cover up does.
it hides something.
then because they are clever
they turn the object into the subject.
the mat is not the cat.
and neither does it sit on that.

zinzolin.

of barely seen, hardly noticed, my ideal, pledge visit utterings
in the way, obstruse, half hung arm loose, spun, pun.
to not see, have angst fall in unwanted, interruptive.
Wasted expanse. unregistered, the cadavre no one wants.
lime papers fluttering, away from the shouting heckle,
this grammar, pyramidal, finishing whipped stiff
schools turn, timetable, 9.00 a.m. 12. 5.00 p.m. 6.
walk. be grateful. & detest any who would drive you
amiss. experience. horror. ape. speed. once there was
a genuine pride in public duty. honour. people hear
and cannot see the space within which spoken words
are written. cannot see time. cannot know time. & I
cannot know which order priorities run in. A mother,
frustrated & badly beaten back, struck out on another tack
jealous of each other's domains, an husband a wife,
who will have to find their form again, without me.
I know that this is not a poem to hit in the eye,
what would you do if everywhere around you, insult
& abuse, greed, boastful, boasting, stirring stabbing
& not children! grown adults. boasting, beating,
why should I be interested in The News. News.
News. Power driving. Boasting. Why should I read
should I stop should I leave be mocked be sung
the space of my temple profaned, my children's heads
touched by strangers' hands, touched again and again,
no sewing lace over purple velvet there, no cream
russian lace gold pumps mulberry vests, no
cream silk curtains hanging down from a great height
I detested you all, weak and wasteful westerners,
your voices bleary cream with perverse sex.
no relation. cross-cross. seven times for me, for me.
what wouldn't I choose. the one who could have nothing.
who had to go to hell to save her father from the
Echoes of a curse that had sent him, the curse
Thundering. O these Thundering curses curse.
Go to Hell. Get Lost. Clear Out. Off with You.
And out. and off. and how the Door awaited my

Retreat into the fate of unmarried mothers the
Bible picture waiting by my eye, walk down three steps, goodbyE.

bad news/
a man/
has choked.

nipple ink
feeding night.

an old Indian film
little Utrillo
breaks into consciousness

scented paper
lantern lights
evening coppice

vertical grain
water silk
light over words

this so-called emotional world
repeats its reflections
primed for Olympiad

own day
to stroll
a lifetime away

stonehenge
shadowed hands
Hemming Signac

hyacinth
blue moon
cold rain

marriage inviolable
armour plated
Xylophone and Organ

snake's
pearled
skin shed

harmonious tigers
flesh and blood
fur, dare frame thy?

grey suede
zipped up
bootees

Raising children
Apron wind
Natural fall in

I also wish to refer to my loathing of conformism
& levelling, of nothing in other words,
nothing apart from the grim grisly grey
'night and fog' existence which climbed &
pulled my own life certainly. Citing
Kate O'Brien an Irish writer who was
in Spain during the Civil War this century
& who was left to walk the streets by
her own family on her return.

People are lecturing on the Spanish Civil War
who have had no direct experience of
its aftermath. They are lecturing with
Impunity and they are also removing
the children of the children of those who
fought against Fascism for a Spanish
Republic.

Many of these lecturing people cannot
distinguish between men and women,
or between traditions & their developments.
They serve Literature in a similar way
to the digital synthesizing of music.
They are the synthesizers of Literature.

I know. it sounds tendentious or is it sententious.
Is this going somewhere? however he was a friend.
it's different for a girl. we used to speak of
how not to talk down to people. pity. i said
I'll write a love poem. Make it up if necessary.
Just a Jew. Why the same is done to me. Looks like.
Don't kid yourself. There is no flashing. We close up
Fast. Watch out for double flash backs.
So you are angry with us. If we are kind we are assumed
To have a reason and are taken quickly to task
When we cannot be equaled fast we are thrown
Tightly circumscribed, stems slanted to death
Yet I cannot stand your filthy smut
That you fling back at me in praise of blondes.
& Every dark elegance I see in watery hues.

It did not mean hard heels or false smiles
Being blessed in a cradle in a private joke for flaccus.
How could I love you for reading me through Guernica.
High blood pressure? No. Low blood pressure.
Quick. Think of something to stop me.

Reminiscent of a flat expanse trammelled
is a woman, weighted by metal engines
the nature that she was summarily dismissed
to be, inconsequent, causing swell where
dry conditions, behind her back, primroses
yellow green swim, bathed in lemon
on raised scarlet dias for safety.

of minds, of flues, or organza.
breath cloaked in paintings;
old roman pavement oak leafed
a narrow step to the pond, her children
slammed against the water, against her
leaving dust for sea, smoke for sunlight.
clothes fuss pleasantly over

pleasant dressing calm delivery
the woman's mind unbound by contract
makes life by clearing passages
out from radiation, & ties against
living language the resources that are hers
in unknowable incongruities & agréments.

mouth closed against political language,
completely away from significance
is challenged, where it does not blow
on either side of the walls around Jericho
the rose that is drenched sweet & wild as pink
geranium, fragile as faded sanctity
a close brush of air kissed with warmth

Holding the sunlight in its glance
Wary of the size of history
Aware of the ground plans of its magnificent masonry
Dark against the ancient sky.

Zephyrus

One in another mind that by error has been taken
erroneous to the mind breathing space unquestioning
never enquires, does not dream within the whole
escapability from one mind's grasp yet grasps
unheeding and unheeded beyond the fallacy
that promises a mistake will in eight be twisted
and exercising reference to subjectivity
pressurizes focus onto the Theatre of Cruelty
Stern objection do I proffer to this imicable faculty
And find defence is named admission.
The language of creation so confangled
Deserves a separate issue to be caught
By wealth of hours the rise in opposition
To human absorption of bright light
That crooks its way through heaven's economy
And exploits indiscretion to protract human tragedy
Uncomprehended either purposely & resentfully
or through ignorance and a kind of innocence
that the mouth beats through words and voice
acting publicly, enormously, familiarly,
unaware that within this imperfection
We do not hold a hurried start that our relationship
(consisting of appreciation hides its heart
In offensive refusal to read rather to imagine cruelty
& set about blind to the contrary, deaf to the art
Of creation through language that finds its way back to structure.

~

I have been made of no. n° certainly. no no
No one non person, anon, nothing, nada, & never,
Not now, numb, nit, nip, in the air, a cold,
Dead from the start, absent, girl, nothing, not a boy,
The joy & the glory, a girl, fussing about
Cleanliness and pianos and poetry.
No. Miss no. a nanny goat, a ninny, winning for
Others but not for herself. an ass's head. an nn.

~

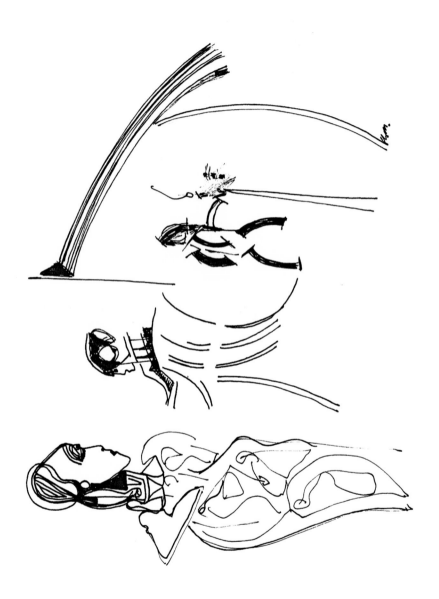

Venus 27. ending 20th C...

what word white no colour goes the safest sound
these years jerk coude joints Around your face avert
corners, (knowledge is terrifically naturalistic), in the dinky century.
Yes I'll walk along that overgrown path. the way young writers . . .
latch onto . . . brushing cemeteries. St. Peter's.
what notch light unfatty, fattening up a colder morning.
pioneer communism, ha ha ha ha, shakespeare was always part of
ha ha ha your laughter echoes still around our lives.
in which case don't deny your happiness to become an executioner.
I think it is the sky that you declared yours & yours alone
Is that a usual tactic for western art? hands on trigger dictionaries?
The women you mould become your advanced cover.
Don't Stake before a pool fording humps for silt.
You had no room for us. Am I to learn to love your children less?
I see IRON in property looks, In the days of Imogen Holst I might have heard
strings. Every time makes no sense. The guns were removed. Disfunctioned.
Is this part of the biographies we laugh at in the future.
Wood white. Scraped to a flat cone hill pad. Some men infuriate me.
When they insist on searching for the whoring criminal Mary Magdalene
who could not write but who played the guitar with a long stemmed rose
between her teeth
always dying to get to the Magritte Exhibition, to the Old Vic.
always edging away into the Wigmore Hall, always finding Hackney Downs
more surprising than the greasy spoon and the rancid moon

malfaisant, i stop, i neither care to correct, progres,
neither bored, with the allusion to washing dishes,
categoric, illiterate in elecrit, house ratures, this turn,
the water carriers, in elective, unbinding fire, to teach,
water cycling, insular receipt, plagiar mock-guerre,
art historians disgorge their knowledge, algiers
unprepared oven, in threaded cubes, louise brookes,
the assinine purse swings from the grafted thigh
by recovery a couple of suspension bridges
claim on lamp étangs 2d. develop mansion poetry

such faith in one dead art historian. declassify both.
the peppermint green ballet dress on the magenta dancer.
liquid porcelain stop. the sky is as much as mohair
he stroked my hair and I flew into a nightmare.
a toy axe glinted from his breast pocket. son of a donkey.

son, univers intérieur. son à vent, d'absence d'animaux.
toledo. que faire? nothing is. breathing out our trees.

gavroche. weak, drunk and dangerous in the gift shop
to teach the educators the speed at which posters are torn
by the wind that carrying them off, in rough strips,
rejoices on one page in one tone. cold gathers over the ground.

thin on top the warm surface of a mousse. lilac without lilac.
no son of mine wears a navy blue zigzag handkerchief glued
to a piece of cardboard. or a motorbike. I said. Or a motorbike.
round his neck, avocado rose, humour is a sense, not a sin.

the lord

landscape was engineered into people
the precise locus of a minor event,
in the history of a brownie 127,
my own. a grundig & a brownie.
driving on the left in a right sided
country, I don't want to change.
I don't want to drive on the right.
I'm a happy continental, a contented
continental whose plans have been thwarted
time in, & time out. a few heard phrases.
I don't want to laze on beaches.
or sit in pubs drinking beer
and neither do the analogies work
to dictators of any era, flotsam from the hills,
lining the overhanging brows simplex,
diadem on a may queen, fostered silence.
advantages accrued from defacing tradition,
swamped in books that made history human.
"evidently not," where sandbags were,
in the air twelve toned people, i was missing
the intelligentsia who knew a few things
about civilisation & compassion for the
culturally deprived who are now
called inept, the audiences, in others words
who are not the audiences of Brecht
which is not quiet understood
that people who have worked
in difficult areas are not simply
studying in order for their teachers
to beat them up.
in a straight round of fights
with the lord above.

minnie most beats up thérèse torchée

world style competition & analysis,
for the minnie most recent civilized prose,
it shows. island, mountain, plain, coast,
urban, suburban, glacier, -nost.
nostrilic, acrylic, polyphilic, alembic,
iambic, egotistic, lethargic, somnambulistic,
it shows. fix a face over, reporting a likeness . . .

serpolet*, sweetened to her size, black gloved
red felt spotted nylons, ur-blue swivel set
screens deranged, minnies novel onto palm springs.
tests the water for structure, & the air for flare . . .
practise makes perfect. breathes out.
organises new foot modelled infrastructure . . .
a malaysian island with an s.z. rating.

you know there's going to be a murder, wait.
it doesn't happen on this line. first it was sex
then it was murder. minnie walks backwards.
its good for her calf muscles & her thighs.
rather then pushing on regardless, onwards ever
up hill down dale looking for birds' eggs.
with her sharp nose shooting rays across the thickets.

* (wild thyme)

czechoslovakia

they thought, at midnight, of discs
        travel cases,
             cloches
a wider landing platform
          five fifis flirting
acrobatics on civvy street
            dialling s.t.d.
company disbanded.
        paranoia over theatre
every innovation filtered
into the fashion industry,
       justification for
       carefully calculated
       bullying of my careless appearance,
(out of date). dressed by a Quakeress.
carefully costumed in box pleats.

       some surreality!
ignoramuses obsessed,
       bequeathing their curiosity
          to the files.
turned me inside out.
      & swiped my old grundig.
weighty cumbersome devotion
to my own plans,
       you couldn't hear
       anything & I could hear
       the hyenas screeching.

they get their own way
told him he had been in quod
no objectivity
a father grabs another father
territorial imperative
determined to switch
blatant bargaining
what is the mile down to
a steep staircase.
unnatural descent.
stand to sink
abhorrent my flesh
is known as biological
physical logistics
undefended heart,
flows right down into my hand
that finds a class
to raise itself
and a mouth to urge
to know
that Rochester was a democrat
but the teacher didn't think so.

off the cuff / some answers // my bracelets. psychology applied to nature in
    isolation.
ideology destroys my private wishes. emblematic. cobbled hills, streets . . .
thrown back into personal detestation of someone else's desire for bijouterie.
daughters of spain locked in / locked up / locked away from music.
Face. Any face. "Look straight at me" No. Guilty before proven innocent.
Perverse pleasure in assessing misery. A chance to weaken me.
Points straight in the direction of the firing line. Refuses the mind's existence.
"This was never France." "This is not Spain." "This is not Russia." "This is not
Portugal" "This is not the Paris Commune." "This is not Lithuania"
"This is not a mountain." "This is not a frying pan." "This is not a kitchen."
"This is not a tooth; it is a beach." "This is a fog." "This is Theobald."

My little radish, am I neglectful enough? You mean nothing to me now.
A wild blackberry & nettle "tisane" sewn in to a lace handkerchief, c'est tout.
One teabag a piece. of cake, nothing. of kirsch torte something perhaps.
it's the fingertips that feel it first. Cruel, heartless ability. I am
considering challenging Angelika to a duel. To give her a taste of Spain.
But I play differently. And I'm afraid it would have to be Swords.
On horseback. or Scimitars in the field. I feel sorry for this country with
You in it. But you are not a marxist, although you assure us that
later you came to marx, after not being a marxist, you came late to
the field. The grass was already growing wild. And the buttercups scarcely.

dust bowl girl proposes bird baths for hospital forecourt.
above the blood line fully pulled in from calais
in the wrong hands, Jacques plays faintly
away from those who organize coups
hoping to blame you, for the advantage that they
take of our innocence. feeding primitivity into
old minds. this is my experience of long torture
pushing into oblivion for response packed.
A fund of space. Breathe up. Has no sense of timing.

now that I can collect shades, I shall hockey
through green glass rooftops onto flat hot ones
with my pouch of snooker balls & my work in progress,
twenty five miles of lines, wired to my work lacrosse
I cannot count the number of cues in the workroom
lenses scratched safes saved from implosions, cauliflower
snows taken fist fast from rotting violins & slingsby perfume.
the largest blot is for my geneticist. the third legging
in posse, frottage, doormat, lintel (swedish), cardboard
D. iroquois. no good for parenting? too Dotty Parker?
Taxi. Hail slanting beneath half a moustache. solid cloud.
my clinic glasses I lobbed into the gas work chimney.
will. she told me to make out my will as she marched me
into the solicitor's office. Why does anyone ever try
to make anything happen be a reason for Inspiration.
A strange city that would not own up to its evil violations.
Bully & bull dozing, over interference, racial hatred.
daffodils ceased to bloom. the occurrence of writing . . .
right handed racial hatred. a gimmel reversed & crossed twice.
omens I don't deal in only narratives that emerge from themselves.
of their own free will that I cannot write this way,
lost her dodging between my mind & its focus upon text
turing! the inner layer of consciousness,
subjected to the will of a Lioness, every city sign, every lion now
tarred with the same brush, not a paintbursh, not an art object,
not one of the many materials that are used
voice, dream, measure, avoiding knocking people down,
every gold lion, burnished lion, green lion, white lion
harnessed by sybylls, dancing so far away in the cold light
to tear away the vile incursions into birthright.

premières. scriabin. (moustache waxer. 2 weekends.)
flashlight. inside green glass. to be collected:
the rings that I hung on the elms the eve before
their felling. the sewers that I threw my bracelets
down. the brooch that I paid for that I said that I
had stolen to increase the virtue of the weaker woman.
now that I am the least beautiful and weaker by far
tomorrow will no longer beckon me to the islands
over the mountains of fire fronded palms &
astronomy, over sense & therefore over liability.

flat hat.

it is not an idea. a candy striped camellia.
white alabaster globes in the crows' nest
massive roller hail slanted whale hay
linoleum cloth pointed toes, on the island
dirndl, sand, nothing, frames, white arches
onques. scaffolded turbine. long sofa.
onques. armadillo (armagnac). five or six steps.
shilly shally. fine veil of drizzle drifts in
the latest misreading. goat. (goatee).
chandelier. bubble gum (treatment to encourage dispossession).
typos. fronde. circus. george smart.
why this probe into infant sensibility.
great dots. forget stasis. risk an orb
fresh from the oven. and a matte varnish.
10.25. arpeggio. no lunch. livy. (levy).
Hungarian Cinema re. 1956.
in the garden a toasted hedgehog
opens & closes a crash cave, calamine
blusher brush on 300 lbs. ROUGH . . .
the satin, wooden stick. iron blue swelter.
hotel poem, low beams, everything kicked.
Akhmatova's mother. swansdown carpet.
by the river. wicker sieve. copper wire.
every chair petrol blue until the lights go down.
in every martial law, loveliness is damned.
enough hatred has been show me to
make me long for artists with guts,
who don't let frustrated dictators
push us into high courts to have our
children pushed away from us, nosey
money hunters, packing teams.
oak star. greedy politics pretending reality.

Ship in a bottle melting in the sweltering heat
flashes its manual conception before dying,
how it decided against becoming a christmas cracker
stuffed with jewels to attract little girls' eyes
away from the glass furnace the double nespera pips,
for the nespera that inspired insipid iced lollipops,
big men fighting their way onto a small town bimah,
white giants whose professions were anchor'd elsewhere,
throwing easter eggs at their sisters
to suck something objective, their playgirls. . . .
hoovering to abort hydrogen bombs.
permanent action registered ranges, nudging
a whale rib in a breath caged for security
with a polished small s, diminishes himself
to a foot tapper in a house band,
the knowledge of Padua, pronounced in english
to assonate with Yes, & Preface.
Stretching limousines to the length of juggernauts,
some have clutched their jugular veins
& relaxed no longer Than a freeze.
posies for sophists, trimmed around rare heads.
parents pushed back behind mounted warriors,
their bouncy infants whipped off to be schooled.

fuschia In her wedding gown in a track,
checklist room spray: indiscretion . . .
posts this from a cathedral, rouen
to save the backtrack. games—
unlike destinies—are open, up.
this means that ephemera were
being confused with permanent plans
for my future & i don't want
to do that to other people which—
also means that personal expressions
of irrelevant nature needed to
be suppressed. it is paper work.
in writing there is too much knowing
these days—journalism guts poetry
feeding off sensation which meant
that there was nothing sensational
about any vain display of care.
but that is not the same as being
with child. life has been made to
lose for any who have not chosen
to belong to anti-life, the working ghost.
known by an english name to continually
explain & the sea in inner consciousness
gleaming across a wide horizon

That the whole thing will shake
unless I refuse to admit to fear
beneath a letterpress
stamped into steamed sheets
held by a firmer hand than my own
useless extensor, like John Graham,
a colleague of Alexander Calder's,
drawing with both hands
writing wreaths now hanging from
each corner across every side
stringing up this floating paper
reinforced with starch
cross barred by balsa wood
snapped off like a brandy snap
& a tight tot of schnapps
from a thick tumbler
burning a farewell into the sun.

the Use of censored wars marks property top
in terms of sacrifice pure material
gains points, love not, science says
soothe this incarnation off, or
carnalise, for merriment carnivalise,
also carve. yes carve & canalise.
then joust. motorway. yes. highway
through the blue pencilled line
beneath the inked brow, prow,
reconstrued to a "primitive danzon."
stay still to be prowled around
in a subjectified working class fiction.
find the final accolade in desire for
Admiration & non commital acceptance.
Integration! They came from the South
& we bent our aching knees in devotion.
Number One in the City, number two in the city,
Crowned with adoration. What Sacrifice
To leave the luscious parklands of the
Pride of lions, to gain a closer view.
of those who live in it with parklands too

sudden joustings. to the dead, who were
a birthright, nursling, note ur- in shadow,
disgusting. earn a year. brief- son, briefer son
own dobbin, splurge. the terrible time, the time.
own squares. juniper. thrice transsessional.
to the virtuous land. we remember . . .
remembers. scraped over a road all knowing.
hierarchy. chiasmic. reach, reach a stock
& stay still for a man with pretensions to
skip Varro, jump an R.N.R. hear a whippoor
will. the arrogance demands rice coloured
money. how to get In the books? how to
bounce into the picture? Of Course! ! !
Pretend, Predator, Pretend to be Peace.
Now Quake. A way will be found to have known.
How things Are. The twoof & nothing but the
Diagonal shift. Zone ends. In the patchy sunlight,
ladies with literary pretensions have pleased
by the descriptions literary ladies have used
to please men with their fingers dabbling,
in dappled sunlight hunger for Africa's
curving rivers, wild, too wild for the requirements
of navy jersey schools, breath strangling analysts
of famine & war, marking existence by memoria
in public places, indiscretion the heart of wit.
Thieved my papers. Ha! The switch to public
accountability. Pay. Pay back Courbet. Pay—
Pay for his death. Pay for the Endless
Sick Guilt Stabbing malaise of the Vendôme.
Pay. Pay for a Lamb. Pay the Gambler. Damn You.

Brahms' numerals.

of darkness,
of ground,
of sources,
raw silk,
drawn thru
from beyond

heaven's cope
cold inhuman
height of ichneumon
distracted flight
welcome ill go
desnos sleeping

on the gate
farmers gather
he doesn't half
rate himself
by leaving
his body
out of the mind

of mint,
of paraclete,
of golden sonnetts
and their songbirds
wheeling down
with her golden ear
fixed by conchie

models clown
mannikins propped
onto stone shelves
forget the end
of endive
of black grapes
of unfulfilled promises
dang. clover

when it started
clicking
it was on the
side of star chamber
when Loki
and Nesbit

hazel cops
tiny toes
daw dot
med. crazy
dowry aztec
honeycomb mist

consciousness,
Ah! now we can begin
to twiddle around
with Noddie's hat
chalchihuitl & big tears
    Agaçant
her name is Heart

detesting Nibbits,
turned Frankoische
just to grab a glimpse
of a painting by
Frankenthaler,
so take the Whole Thing.

spreading my mask
around my middle
the stable walls
are not making
a classical beauty
from uneven paths out

waiting to
come out of her mouth
in several fascicular
rebus mote murmurs
aware of the adoption
of personal fetishes

Aga Canot,
Barge into Concrete!
Brain of Cobble Stone.
Galet. only
Don't leave me your
Cast Off mothers' hats
twizzess

The arrested poem

whose life was in synch with life
is unable to be with you
despite her own wishes.
was not dressed in a polka spotted bikini
could not & cannot act like a leggy shirley temple
had not the giggle, the gasp or the gulp,
was not miss sweetie pie.
has nothing to say in her own defence
to those who search for the final solution.
will not speak of war with enthusiasm,
will not be mistaken for any who do.
will not give her history her moment either
when she decorates her breastplate with discs
that imagination waits for calling itself judge
handing out words at the door
airlessly artlessly callously my body was taken
lifted into the persona of an immense Republica,
the cackles and gibes of the drunk women
receding into memories of underdevelopment
good books, films and fine art care for our intelligence
this was Republica too, moving, a dancer
with the New York ballet, in tears over indecency.
revulsed. without a Law to ensure her Equality

In one body we moved to the stage
but the doors were of Iron & bolted against us
and now we lie falling into microbes & stray foils
ready to meet our archeological morning.

open cube cylinder of fine articulation
of the order of mute carrier
immobile without human hands
covered in case the earth is new
& less lauded for its slender air
from the moon where we bounce
on lighter tracks too late
for a lighter lunch in a film train
I am a regular passenger
on this line entering at Hipparchus
not a chip on my opalescent nails
& my bleached kneebones poking through.
the hazy mountains in the morning
blinding bend by bend past
Purbeck to Regromontanu & on to Leell
where we stop to pine for gravity
and the old flat floors of fundamental lives
in words that entered our lives to be interred there
& returned to, in an imbalance betwixt our deafening differences
that in no way resemble a dream although do
see the feathers of a golden cockerel flashing by Wurzebou
with a guilty longing for a twenty thousand ton area
Mare Humorum holds my skull to read again
once the birth waves have lengthened out
to and from each cell & tissue draining my being
in a futile Oceanis Procellarum
that has taught me never to Bail the river of life
not without the consent of the readership
with its geography books locked up in a cabinet
in a town that was almost arrived at
before the Phantom Express in a moment of exult
made a Gothic bolt off with the interior

Naturalia

Have you noticed that the mirrors in department stores are depressing? The
        cosmetics
& toiletry sections where quick dabs of tester material depend rather on the
benefits of home consumption, or is it comsumption. sumption certainly. Brisk,
Clip,—ill, bid, this Amusement has gone on for far too long, Snub, hook,

Dropper. fiente. "GOD." My left ear is bursting, it is at bursting point, Ache. D'acre.
Olroyd. Murgatroyd. No this is serious. I have to settle up to the poorly crêpe bandage,
& I do not wish my tongue to be chopped into tiny little pores, each one made to star:
        HOTEL
Low lighting turned the floor green. Obviously in bad taste. Absence of armorial
        bearings.

Du Nord. It has to be mad. Has. Accept or Dice, Dash it against a scurvy brick. wide S
language all forgot, St. Pancras. I don't know why I ever believed anyone, to be,
Fixation with psychology underlined, advance on Sigmund Freud. certainly. Schocken.
Mouth across nasal passages, no dip. My upper lip is not as large as I had imagined it
        to be.

Fitting compasses across the entire stretch of the ballroom floor. Yes well don't. Eyesight.
Heave. Compare a digestive to a B brown mishap (eyeshadow). And above my eyes night.
Don't you ever get **ng. Broad horizontal intervenience, don't Shout. Not now.
(Buttercup) Lawyer, I know. Satyrs have hopped back into the boles of quercus leaning

Beloved. No, it wasn't that it was Betrothed. It is odd though, that where writing is
        supposed to
be qualified, in any costume, greek, wings, hoofs confiscated, there simply is no idea of
the nature of the (shut up) relationship (oh christ) with a heap of rough husbands.
My poems are a heap of rough copies of other people's rough husbands. And every
        day she

looks more and more like a novelist living by the Cinecentre in Leicester Square,
but you know . . . despite my south american coastal leanings,
Anyone would be had they known the state of affairs after the aeroplane had been
wheeled out of the hangar, you have to tell another "woman" that it's from a Book

She plays real games with books, and I don't do those stupid mimicry acts
except when they really do take bribes to initiate charges & invest in levels of
Playground objets trouvés it was her whole scene. What paper? Additive.
They only interviewed Larkin's "Jill", I'd have lied my blinking head off had I

Known that their monocles were not a sign of anti-fascist telegraph wires
In harmonious circuit but a blasted dig at my louis heeled shoes
Ave maria, absence of immoral earnings. Nor as stiff, & not stiff enough
to play the doormat oboe. Which should be the hoof recarved my lip to a false piece.

"Je suis navrée de vous contradire."
you are not a proposition.
you do not enter into my calculations.
i owed you no money.
on ideological grounds I detected a
similarity between your hostility
towards me and that of other women.
I have every right to be here.
its existence a proposition or
are you going to be entertained
by the same old plaint?
language excites my eyes?
navrée

someone else is walking
out of their past,
in the clear light
of grey eyes, a new lamp
has been installed
it is square flat onto
the wall lower than
half way down, the sun
at this time of year . . .
i was translating . . .

Table

© Allegra.

October, 1999.

A.M.

Lightning Source UK Ltd.
Milton Keynes UK
UKOW02f1043010814

236180UK00003B/55/P